Grandpa's

Safari

Written & Illistrated by Terri Page

Colorist & Finish Artist: Tessa Page

Dedicated to my husband,

who not only allows me to dream,

but helps me make my dreams

a reality!

When we go to Grandpa's house, we know it will always be an adventure! Grandpa is always working on something.

Grandpa likes it when we help him work. He says that we are big helpers!

After his important work is done, we go on a safari! (Just to make sure that Grandma and her berries are safe.)

We have to wear special glasses when we go on our safari. They are "im-agin-ation" glasses! Ready? Let's go!

We hold Grandpa's hand because he wants us to. We never know what we will find. "Look!" says Grandpa, pointing across the creek.

"A Lion!"

We looked really hard, but all we could see was Mopsy, the neighbor's fluffy dog.

Grandpa had us adjust our special glasses. It would be fun to see a lion, but we were really glad it was Mopsy!

Just then we heard a noise behind us. "What is that?" I asked. Grandpa turned around and said, "I think it's a tiger!"

We held Grandpa's arm and scooted behind his back.

We don't like tigers! Not in Grandpa's back yard.

"Grandpa, that is Stripes, he belongs to your other neighbor!"
We know Stripes very well. He came up and let us pet him.

We were getting worried about Grandpa. We didn't think that
his glasses were working. When we told him, he smiled and
took our hands to walk over by the blackberries.

This is our favorite spot, because Grandma has raspberries and blackberries here. We get to pick them when they are ripe.

Grandpa grows pumpkins here too! Just before Halloween, he will let us choose a pumpkin from his special patch.

"Stop!" Grandpa held our hands tight. Just then we heard a noise in front of us. We had scared something and it moved. There, in the berries, was a deer. Grandma would not like that. The deer was eating the leaves on Grandma's plants. The deer jumped the fence without any trouble and was soon across the canal. They sure run pretty.

We went to see how much the deer had eaten. Suddenly, up flew lots of birds. Grandpa said they were quail.

They have funny things on the top of their heads. That's how we know what they are. They eat Grandma's berries too!

Grandpa said it was time to sit in the tree house. He brought his "bon-ac-u-larz." We are going to look for more animals hiding in the field.

It didn't take long before we spotted something orange. We pointed at it for Grandpa. He used his "bon-ac-u-larz" and said, "Good job buddy!" That's what Grandpa calls us all of the time. What do you think we saw?

Yes! We saw a fox! We like seeing them when we are safe in Grandpa's tree house!

One night we decided to stay up late and look at the stars. It was just getting dark. We laid on the grass close to Grandpa. We were looking up at the sky, when all of the sudden something really big came towards us.

A Great Horned Owl! He swooped down close to us and then went back up into the air. It was quiet and pretty.

After the owl left, we smelled something yucky! It got really stinky outside.

Grandpa laughed when we pinched our nose. He said it was just a skunk passing by the back fence and that we should leave skunks alone.

It's sad that they are so stinky. They look very soft and cuddly.

We asked Grandpa if he had ever seen a hedgehog. We were hoping we could see one of those too.

He said we will only find pet hedgehogs in America. The ones that are wild and free live in other countries.

Suddenly we saw something jump in the canal. "Is it a whale?" I cried.

Grandpa smiled and said, "No, it's a catfish."

"Look Grandpa! A monkey!"

Grandpa smiled and said, "No, it's just a squirrel."

We told Grandpa that he needed to adjust his "im-agin-ation" glasses now. He smiled and said, "You're right!"

Just then, something hopped behind us. "What is it?" We asked excitedly. "Just a magpie." said Grandpa.

We both looked at Grandpa and told him to look again.

He smiled and adjusted his glasses. "A rabbit?" he asked, looking all around him.

We told Grandpa to try one more time! He smiled and looked really hard. "Is it brown?" he asked.

"Are you talking about that Kangaroo behind you?"

We both jumped! We didn't see the kangaroo until Grandpa did. Now we know that Grandpa's glasses are working.

We were talking about the thing jumping in the water.
(Sometimes we have to give Grandpa a hint.)

"A frog?" he asked.

"No Grandpa, it is much bigger than a frog. And it can be very dangerous!"

"Does it have big teeth?" he asked.

"Yes, and a very big mouth!" we cried.

Oh." said Grandpa, "Do you mean my pet crocodile? I call him Fred."

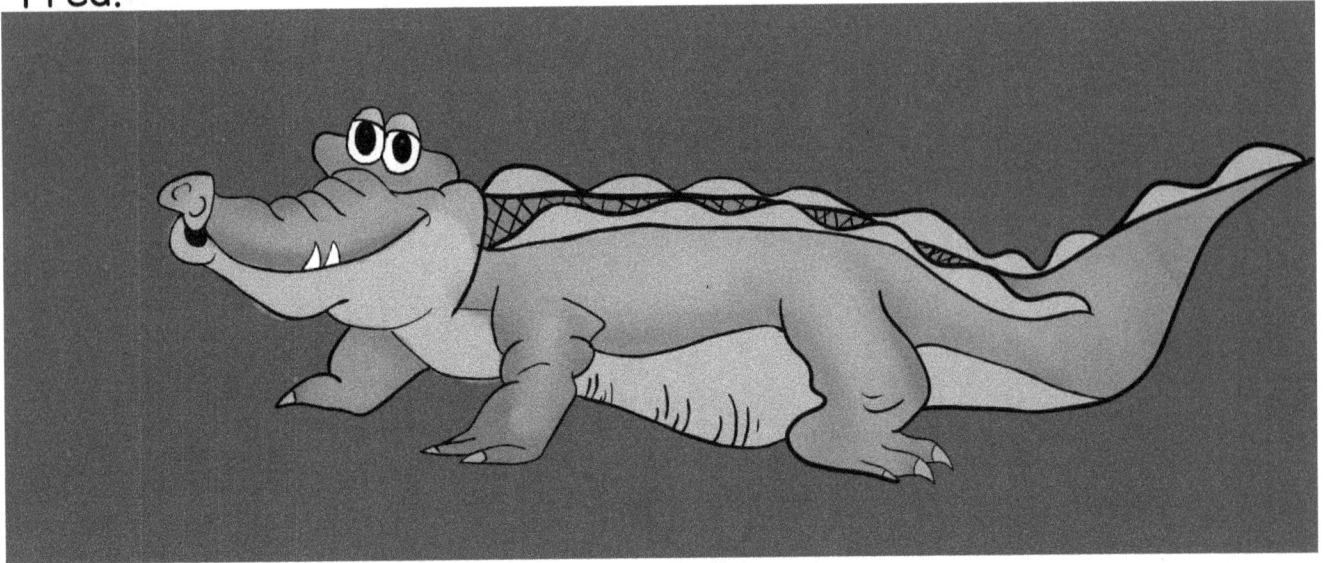

"Or were you referring to Hannah?" "Who is Hannah?" we asked Grandpa. "She is over there, in the canal. Hannah is Grandma's pet hippo."

We laughed so hard that we made a snorting noise. Grandpa was still laughing when he picked up the "bon-ac-u-larz." "I just heard a snort. Can you find the wild boar?"

"I don't think it is a pig, Grandpa. I think it is a rhino!" We all took turns with the "bon-ac-u-larz." None of us could find the rhino.

Just then, we heard Grandma calling us to come and get a Popsicle. Grandpa said, "Don't tell Grandma what we saw back here today. It will make her scared. She doesn't wear "im-agin-ation" glasses anymore."

We laughed and said, "Oh yes, she does Grandpa! Have you ever seen her talk to her flowers, especially the Pansies?"

What lives in your back yard?